Original title:
Life: What's the Point of It All?

Copyright © 2025 Creative Arts Management OÜ
All rights reserved.

Author: Matthew Whitaker
ISBN HARDBACK: 978-1-80566-128-3
ISBN PAPERBACK: 978-1-80566-423-9

The Irony of Our Shortcomings

We strive for gold but trip on dust,
With broken shoelaces, we learn to adjust.
In a world of chaos, we clutch at our dreams,
Yet, often, we fumble — or so it seems.

We climb up mountains with our arms full of snacks,
Only to find that the view's got no cracks.
Laughter fills the air as we stumble and sway,
For every big plan, we've a comical play.

A Flicker in the Vastness

A candle's glow in the universe wide,
We seek to shine, but often we hide.
In search of answers, the stars are our guide,
Yet, sometimes we trip over our own pride.

We wave at the moon, while our socks don't quite match,
With cosmic curiosity, we hatch and we catch.
In this grand theater, a flicker's a blast,
Being goofy as starlight? It's all unsurpassed.

The Undefined Horizon

A horizon appears, but is never so clear,
We squint and we ponder, with a laugh or a sneer.
With maps of confusion, we plot out our path,
Yet detours in life always trigger a laugh.

We wander through fields of unkempt grass,
Chasing the clouds as they drift and they pass.
In the grand game of charades, we play our part well,
For every missed goal, there's a joke we can tell.

Searching for a Silver Lining

In every gray cloud, we search for a gleam,
With umbrellas of hope, we dare to dream.
Yet puddles of laughter often slip through our shoes,
Life's a game of chance, we laugh at the blues.

A rainbow appears, or so we hope it will,
But it's more like a prank that gives us a thrill.
As we chase after rainbows, we trip here and there,
Finding joy in the chaos, that's half of the dare.

Whispers of the Unseen

In the corner, socks conspire,
Dancing dreams, a laundry fire.
Coffee spills on plans we make,
While the cat plots our next break.

We chase shadows, pretend to soar,
Stumbling through an open door.
Tickles find us in our sleep,
Giggling secrets we can't keep.

Fragments of a Fading Day

Chasing dusk on roller skates,
Try to juggle all our fates.
Once we thought we had it locked,
Now we laugh as fortune mocked.

With a wink, the moon peeks shy,
Winks at us, as time slips by.
Count the stars, they seem to jest,
Whispers say, 'Just take a rest.'

The Canvas of Our Days

Brushstrokes bright, then dull and gray,
Splash of mischief in the fray.
Colors of a morning greet,
While we search for missing feet.

Our canvas yields both joy and grime,
Yet we dance, ignore the time.
Cupcake crumbs on walls we trace,
Artful chaos, our embrace.

Wandering Through the Unanswered

Questions linger like a breeze,
Whistling softly through the trees.
Maps are drawn in melted wax,
As we laugh at silly hacks.

But the cosmos chuckles loud,
Catering to our jesting crowd.
Finding joy in missing screws,
Poking fun with all the blues.

The Echo of Wandering Souls

In a world of daily grind,
We search for what we've left behind.
Socks unmatched and dreams so bright,
Who knew wrong turns felt so right?

Chasing shadows, what a race,
Finding joy in every place.
With laughter echoing our way,
We dance through night, ignore the day.

Threads of Existence

We weave our tales with silly threads,
In coffee spills and snack-filled spreads.
Why worry 'bout the grand design?
Let's stick with pizza and some wine!

Each hiccup leads to zany fates,
Like ducks that play at open gates.
While pondering if this is real,
Just grab a snack, it's a good deal!

The Weight of Unasked Questions

Why do ducks always quack at night?
And does our laundry take flight?
The mysteries pile as we just grin,
    Maybe it's a cosmic spin!

What's with the sock thief, so unkind?
He steals our sanity, peace of mind.
But in confusion, there's a spark,
    Let's chase the giggles in the dark!

Sunsets and Silhouettes

Watch the sun drop, a golden show,
While we laugh at what we don't know.
The silhouettes dance on the ground,
With pirouettes, they spin around.

Each setting sun, a chance to jest,
As twilight gleams and shadows rest.
So in the glow, let worries flee,
Embrace the fun, just let it be!

A Canvas of Dreams and Doubts

In a world of paint and brush,
We wonder, 'Why the rush?'
Colors blend, then fade away,
We laugh, oh what a silly play!

A canvas filled with splats and spots,
Is it art or just some blots?
With every stroke, we ponder more,
Could it be a hidden door?

The Compass of Contentment

A compass spinning, what a tease,
Pointing north, then south with ease.
Should I follow where it glows?
Or wander where the wild wind blows?

With each step, the map's unclear,
But hey, at least there's cold root beer!
In circles we go, round and round,
Laughing at the paths we've found.

Chasing the Fading Light

I trot along the sun's last rays,
In search of golden, brighter days.
But shadows dance and giggle too,
    Saying, 'Catch us if you do!'

The light retreats, a playful game,
While I just wander, feeling lame.
With every step, I trip and fall,
But wait, what's that? A free-for-all!

Whispers of Forgotten Dreams

In a closet far away, dusty and small,
Lies a dream that had a ball.
Whispers echo, 'Hey, come play!'
But I'm busy on this sunny day.

Forgotten hopes in dusty frames,
Calling out with silly names.
Should I dance alongside my fears?
Or sip some tea and laugh at years?

A Labyrinth of Perceptions

In a maze of thoughts we wander,
Chasing cheese, but it's just a blunder.
A squirrel's opinion, a frog's debate,
We scramble 'round, oh what a fate!

Giraffes in tuxedos play chess,
While ducks give speeches, none the less.
We laugh as the world spins in glee,
Wondering if we're all just free.

Embracing the Unanswerable

Why does toast land with buttered side down?
Is it just fate, or a cosmic clown?
We ponder and scratch our heads in fright,
As pigeons conspire to steal our bite.

Kittens plot as we chase the car,
And ants parade, dreaming of gold bars.
Questions swirl like confetti in the air,
Perhaps we should just stop and stare.

Through the Veil of Dreams

In dreams, I'm a cat at midnight's call,
Dancing on rooftops, feeling so tall.
Then suddenly, I'm stuck in a shoe,
Wondering if this dream's come true.

A bear plays the banjo, oh so sweet,
While turtles in hats keep a lively beat.
We juggle our thoughts like jellied dough,
In this circus of dreams, we steal the show.

Patterns in the Chaos

A squirrel with a briefcase dashes by,
Declaring that today, he'll reach the sky.
While fish in bowties debate the best style,
As we roll our eyes and chuckle a while.

The universe spins like a dizzy top,
With socks mismatched, will we ever stop?
Patterns emerge from the silly dance,
Reminding us all to take a chance.

Breathing in the Mystery

In the morning, I brew my tea,
Grumbling softly, "What's for me?"
The cat judges from high above,
While I ponder, seeking love.

Shoes on the wrong feet, what a sight!
I trip on thoughts, taking flight.
A jogger laughs as I tumble down,
Hoping to earn a silly crown.

So many roads and paths to roam,
Yet here I am, stuck at home.
An egg and toast, my big delight,
Sometimes it's good to goof all night.

When clouds confound my sunny plans,
I dance with shadows, make new fans.
Through every chuckle, one great truth,
Questioning keeps the heart and youth.

The Complexity of Simple Tides

The ocean sways with wise old jokes,
It laughs at stranding foolish folks.
With every wave, a playful wink,
"You're never lost, just pause to think."

Seagulls squawk, demanding fries,
While time just flows and never lies.
I toss a chip, they dive and screech,
As I reflect on life's strange beach.

Footprints mark the sand, then gone,
Just like my hope for a morning dawn.
Each sunset chuckles, painting skies,
"Now go ahead, try to be wise!"

So here I stand, with sand in toes,
Chasing answers no one knows.
Among the tides, I slip, I slide,
Embracing chaos in the ride.

Not All Who Wander Are Lost

With a map that's upside down,
I wander through this quaint old town.
People smile, I just say, "Hi,"
Like their laughter lifts me high.

The bus stops here, a perfect flare,
But there's naught to catch, not a care.
I'll follow squirrels, hear tales so tall,
Adventure waits, I'll heed its call.

Maybe the compass needs new batteries,
Or I'm just drawn to shady trees.
Each turn, a riddle, I can't resist,
Whisked away by irony's twist.

The sun laughs as I zigzag round,
Finding treasures where I'm not bound.
In this maze with no end in sight,
I embrace the fun, come day or night.

The Pulse of Paradox

I wake up grumpy, dreaming bright,
A cereal box tells me, "Take flight!"
With socks that clash and hair a mess,
I question if chaos is my quest.

Heels on the ground, head in the stars,
I muse about life's silly bars.
Each paradox dances like a tune,
While I wade through the afternoon.

Sometimes I'm wise, sometimes absurd,
Even a snail can find the word.
I dip my toes in puddles deep,
As whimsical secrets dare me to leap.

So let's toast to the quirks we find,
Riddles wrapped in thoughts unkind.
With laughter's breath and a winked eye,
We sip the nonsense, ask "Oh, why?"

A Journey Without a Map

With no direction and no clue,
I wander streets that look askew.
A squirrel points the way I guess,
Maybe I'll find a sweet success.

Chasing shadows, ducks, and pies,
Who knew that clouds could wear a guise?
A stop for snacks, a giggle spree,
I might just lose all sense of me.

The compass spins, it's quite a sight,
I'll dance with joy, ignore the fright.
A journey's fun when steps are free,
Who really needs a map, not me!

So here I am, a happy mess,
Finding joy in all that's less.
I'll skip and hop 'til evening falls,
For fun's the answer, that's my call!

The Weight of Unsaid Words

A thousand thoughts, but lips sealed tight,
I ponder if it's wrong or right.
I practice lines like I'm on stage,
But chicken out, ignite my rage.

My dog just barks 'cause he can't speak,
Yet every glance is just so cheek!
I could convey my deepest fears,
But fear of cringe brings me to tears.

So here's to words that will not flow,
Like turtles swimming far too slow.
I'll keep on smiling, give a wink,
And hope my thoughts don't stink, don't stink!

In the end, it's more absurd,
The weight I bear of unsaid words.
Laugh away the thoughts that bind,
For silence often speaks the mind!

Ramblings of a Restless Soul

Woke up today with a wild stir,
Chasing dreams that eventually blur.
Coffee spills, a sleepy sigh,
Why's it so hard just to fly by?

I've danced with socks and tripped on floors,
Played chess with cats; I'll wage my wars.
The vacuum hums a soulful tune,
I swear it's trying to eat the moon.

Thoughts racing faster than my feet,
Maybe I'll find some lemonade sweet.
Life seems odd, a curious jest,
But who said I must be the best?

So giggle loud, and twirl around,
For laughter's where the joy is found.
With restless soul, I boldly roam,
In every stumble, I find my home!

In the Silence of Stillness

In the quiet, my mind does race,
Am I a genius, or lost in space?
The dark's a friend, my thoughts align,
Plotting to make the stars all mine.

I hear the crickets draft a song,
About the things that feel so wrong.
A squirrel joins, with acorn cheer,
It seems I'm not alone in here!

The world outside may twirl and spin,
But here within, I let joy win.
With every noise, my heart takes flight,
Silence is loud; it feels just right.

So here I sit, a giggling sage,
In the stillness, I turn the page.
Who needs a crowd when calm's the call?
In silent joys, I have it all!

The Question in Every Breath

Why do we chase the rainbow's end?
Is there a pot of gold to lend?
Or just some socks that mismatched clogs?
A world of thoughts, where logic fogs.

We pitter and patter on life's grand stage,
Like a dog with a bone — quite the engage!
Yet, every tick tocks like a clock runs amok,
Chasing the answers, but hit with a shock.

Let's toast to the chaos that calls us near,
To all the odd questions we hold so dear!
With a wink and a smile at the cosmic jest,
We strut on this dance floor, unsure of our quest.

So here's to the puzzling, the jigs, and the fun,
In this wacky parade, we're never quite done!
For each twirl and twist is a thrill to behold,
As we laugh at the stories that merrily unfold.

Chronicles of the Un-asked

What's the deal with the early bird?
Does the night owl think that's absurd?
Do sandwiches dream of being toast?
Questions so silly, yet I love them most.

Round and round, the mind spins on,
As I ponder what's real and what's just drawn.
The cat on the fence, does he clutch his book?
Does he read all about that human rook?

In the theater of thoughts, we giggle and sigh,
With each quirky notion, a question flies high.
Should I dance like no one's at the ball?
Or pretend I'm a tree, standing stiff and tall?

As we scribble our queries in the sand,
Life offers laughter, a quirky band.
So let's hold our breath as confusion spins,
For in these un-asked, the best fun begins!

Between the Lines of Existence

There's scribbles in margins, a curious thought,
What if the universe's just forgot?
A cosmic joke, where we're all the punchline,
So let's laugh it off — we're just fine, we're just fine!

With jellybeans dancing on life's grand chart,
And socks with holes playing their part.
Is fate a dealer with cards up his sleeve?
Or a prankster who says, 'Here's what you grieve'?

Let's sip on confusion, sweet as can be,
And toast to the moments that make us feel free.
If destiny's a course, I'm a ship without sail,
Drifting on whims of laughter and fail.

So in this bizarre script, we play our role,
With gumdrops and giggles, we nourish the soul.
Between the lines, we might just find,
A reason to smile, undefined but kind.

Ciphers of the Universe

Why do we worry about fitting in?
When the stars above just want us to spin?
With patterns like puzzles that twist and shout,
Is there any secret they're all about?

A squirrel in a tie? How dapper he looks!
With acorns as currency in cosmic books.
Do clouds ever wonder what storms will brew?
Or do they just float, saying, 'I'm soaring too'?

A riddle in rhythm, the cosmos plays tricks,
Mixing up galaxies like a jumble of bricks.
Are we players in games we can't comprehend?
With laughter as language that won't ever end?

So let's decode the whispers that tumble so sweet,
In the dance of existence, we tap our own feet.
With riddles and giggles wrapping us tight,
In the ciphers of chatter, we find our delight.

Navigating the Vast Unknown

In a boat with no map, we set out to sea,
With jellyfish hats, as silly as can be.
The stars roll their eyes, in laughter and jest,
While seagulls debate on who's truly the best.

We dodge all the waves like a dance through the sand,
Mocking the fish with our jokes made by hand.
A sunburnt philosopher claims he's got it made,
But all he can offer is lemonade.

Oh, the treasures we seek, hidden deep in the tide,
Turn out to be crabs in a haphazard slide.
Yet still we sail forth, with the wind in our hair,
Clutching our dreams as if they were rare.

As nightfall descends, and the giggles disperse,
We ponder our purpose in this universe.
But then comes a dolphin, with a wink and a splash,
Reminding us lightly, it's all just a laugh.

A Tapestry of Unspoken Thoughts

What's woven in silence can sometimes scream loud,
A blanket of worries, we wrap 'round like a shroud.
But tangled in fibers of whimsy and fright,
We find that our fears are quite silly at night.

The cat thinks he's wise, with his tail held up high,
While plotting a scheme to touch the bright sky.
Yet in chasing the dreams he thinks are so neat,
He trips on his paws and falls flat on his feet.

Each thread tells a story, of both joy and grief,
In colors that clash like a wild disbelief.
Yet laughter can stitch all the ripped seams away,
Making chaos a pattern, come join the ballet!

So dance through the mishaps and trip over bliss,
In this tapestry woven, do not dare to miss.
For each little blunder, each stumble, each laugh,
Is part of the story, a crazy paragraph!

The Weight of Tomorrow's Promise

We wrestle with futures, all wrapped in a grin,
As if tomorrow's banter is waiting within.
With coffee-stained hopes and a toast made of dreams,
We juggle the weight, finding giggles in seams.

The clock ticks like a comedian's old joke,
While plans turn to rubber, all wobbly and broke.
Yet somehow we laugh, with our arms in the air,
Claiming we're artists, painting life without care.

Promises hang by a thread made of cheese,
Each nibble a choice, tickling minds with a tease.
But as we munch on our futures unplanned,
Crumbs fall like secrets, soft laughter at hand.

Tomorrow can wait, while we dance through today,
With silly missteps that lead us astray.
For the weight of the world is a fun, feathery prank,
And who knew a giggle could balance our flank?

Caught in the Web of Wonder

In the tangled-up web where curiosity plays,
We tripped over questions like thorns on a craze.
Each thought a small spider that dances with glee,
Spinning tales of the world that we can't quite foresee.

The sun wears a hat made of clouds and surprise,
While birds plot their heists from the tops of the skies.
We ponder our purpose in this circus of chat,
While the ants throw a party, and we're all invited flat.

With each little wonder, the day transforms bright,
Mysteries dance in the glow of the light.
Why does the grass itch? Why do socks disappear?
The world's a big joke, a serrated veneer.

So let's raise a toast to the absurd and the strange,
Believing in whimsy is how we'll arrange,
A life full of wonders that capture our eyes,
As we laugh at the world and its great big surprise!

The Portrait of Uncertainty

In a world where socks mispair,
I ponder with a goofy stare.
The coffee's cold, my hair's a mess,
Yet, here I am, so full of zest.

The clock ticks loud, yet time is coy,
I search for meaning, chase my joy.
But every ladder's missing rungs,
I laugh it off, my heart still young.

With confusion swirling like a dance,
I trip on thoughts, yet take a chance.
Is breakfast better at dawn or noon?
Who knows, but hey, let's hum a tune!

In the gallery of doubt I stand,
With a paintbrush held in wobbly hand.
I splash on colors bright and bold,
Making paintings out of stories told.

Voices Beneath the Surface

Beneath the waves of daily grind,
Are whispers of the quirky kind.
They tell me tales of socks that flee,
And cats who claim the right of way.

The toaster's popped, my breakfast flies,
As toast escapes in morning skies.
I might just ride a comet's tail,
With jellybeans and my own ale.

There's a circus in my tangled head,
With clowns and thoughts that bounce instead.
They juggle dreams and make me grin,
While gravity says, "Let's begin!"

So here I am, amidst the fray,
Laughing loud at what they say.
In this comedy we call the norm,
I sip my tea and start to warm.

The Absurdity of Certainty

With certainty in every sneeze,
I pen my fate with absent keys.
The cat demands a place to sit,
While I just ponder, "What is it?"

The rules I made are written in sand,
As waves crash down, they slip from hand.
Today I'll dine with spaghetti nice,
Tomorrow's menu? Just roll the dice!

I'll wear mismatched shoes, that's my plan,
While pondering if llamas can tan.
In the land of what ifs, I roam free,
Chasing the absurd, just let it be.

In my silly scheme, I take a ride,
On a rubber duck, oh what a glide!
Each twist and turn, a giggle starts,
In this circus dance, we play our parts.

Trails of Twilight Thoughts

As twilight wraps the world in hues,
I ride a bike with squeaky wheels.
My thoughts paint circles in the sky,
While stars begin their shimmery deal.

Pineapple pizza makes me grin,
Should I swim or just dip my toe?
With questions swirling on a whim,
I follow paths where chuckles flow.

The moon winks down at silly me,
In a dance of shadows, I take flight.
Through tangled leaves, I weave my spree,
Beneath the glow of fuzzy light.

In these twilight trails, I'll find my way,
With laughter echoing as my guide.
For every twist is but a play,
And joy's the treasure in this ride!

Unraveling the Great Design

In the morning, I sip my tea,
Wondering if it's meant for me.
Frog in my throat, is it a sign?
Should I ponder or just feel fine?

Birds above chirp with such flair,
While I contemplate if they care.
Do they know of the plans they make?
Or just hop about for fun's own sake?

I trip on thoughts that float away,
Catch them like leaves in a ballet.
Do the clouds ever think and sigh?
Or just drift along, way up high?

Yet in the chaos, smiles arise,
We dance through questions, oh so wise.
Perhaps it's nonsense, but who's to say?
Let's toast to the silly and call it a day!

Balancing on the Edge of Absurdity

Walking a tightrope of jello beans,
Wobbling like the finest machines.
Why do we struggle to reach the peak?
When ice cream flows like a river creek?

Juggling dreams with a rubber hand,
Who said we need to understand?
I throw my worries to the wind,
Where grassy gnomes with rainbows grinned.

Tickling stars with my bare toes,
Shouting loudly to the cosmos.
"Is this the plan?" I giggle loud,
As rockets launch from a pepper cloud.

In this circus of the grand unknown,
We find the truth in laughter grown.
So let's embrace the weird and wild,
With every thought, let joy be styled!

Threads of Time and Space

In my closet, a sweater stirs,
Spinning tales of what once occurs.
Did my socks negotiate their fate?
Or just vanish, feeling late?

Time is a rubber band stretched wide,
Bouncing back with nowhere to hide.
Do we race or stroll with delight?
As stars giggle in the deep night.

I once met a clock with a grin,
Claiming time's played on a violin.
Notes flutter by like butterfly wings,
In this bizarre dance, laughter sings.

So let's weave the fabric of fate,
With silly threads that we create.
In this tapestry, let's have a ball,
For wondrous moments, we'll cherish it all!

A Symphony of Questions

Gather round for a curious show,
Questions bloom like weeds that grow.
"Why is cheese square and cats just lounge?"
In this mystery, we all can drown.

With each note, the chaos finds form,
Is normalcy hiding in a storm?
Do muffins dream of muffins baked?
Or is it all a joke—fate's pranked?

I asked a cat for the meaning of bliss,
He answered with a purr and a hiss.
"Maybe it's cheese, or naps in the sun?"
In his feline wisdom, he had fun.

So let's hum along to this strange tune,
With giggles and quirks under the moon.
In the symphony of absurd delight,
Questions dance, all through the night!

The Pursuit of Meaning

In a search for the grand, we take sips,
Through coffee-stained maps and comic strips.
With googled advice and smiles so bright,
We ponder our reason by day and night.

Should we chase after gold, or just more fries?
Perhaps in our laughter, true wisdom lies.
As we juggle our dreams like clowns in a show,
The meaning we seek is the joy in the flow.

Riding life's coaster, we scream and we cheer,
While wondering why we are really here.
But amidst all the chaos, one thing is true:
It's fine to be silly, just be you.

So dance like a leaf in the autumn breeze,
And laugh at the questions that tangle like keys.
For in the grand scheme, we may not know,
But having a chuckle is quite the show.

Fragments of Tomorrow's Hopes

We craft our dreams in a wobbly tower,
Built on hopes like sugar, soft as a flower.
With each little tumble, we find a new start,
Questioning futures, we laugh from the heart.

Chasing the sunshine with mismatched shoes,
Wondering if winning is just for the blues.
Hoping tomorrow's not filled with chores,
But filled with ice cream and convenient stores.

We sketch out our plans on napkins and walls,
With doodles of dragons and ribboned balls.
Each fragment we gather, each giggle we save,
Adds color to journeys we happily brave.

So whether we flourish or trip and we fall,
Let's make sure to giggle, that's key after all.
For the fragments we hold in our goofy hands,
Are the sweetest reminders of life's silly plans.

A Tapestry of Unanswered Longings

Woven with threads of our fleeting dreams,
A tapestry tangled with bright, silly schemes.
We stitch and we patch with laughter and glee,
Creating a quilt of what could never be.

As we ponder our passions—woes and delight,
We throw in the towel and start a pillow fight.
In our woven reflections, the patterns seem clear,
It's about sharing giggles with folks we hold dear.

Rusty old hopes can still shine with a flash,
Even if we stumble in life's frantic dash.
Every longing unanswered just adds to the show,
With a sprinkle of humor to lighten the blow.

So let's gather our threads, though we may not see,
The grand design woven perfectly.
With laughter and quirks all sewn in this way,
We'll embrace the unknown and dance through the fray.

Where Footprints Meet the Horizon

With each little footprint upon sandy shores,
We wonder if fate has unlocked all the doors.
Waving hello to the waves as they pass,
We laugh at the questions like curious grass.

Chasing the sunsets, we trip on our toes,
Trying to dance in a world that just glows.
As we peek at the skies with eyes big and round,
We find treasures hiding in laughter unbound.

The horizon is painted with dreams brushed in gold,
And we scribble the stories we long to be told.
When footprints meet waves in a playful embrace,
The point of it all is to simply find grace.

So here's to the fun in each stumble and fall,
To the goofy adventures that beckon us all.
Let's wander together and laugh as we roam,
For the journey itself is our truest home.

Beyond the Veil of Routine

Wake up, yawning, hit the snooze,
Coffee spills, oh what a muse!
Chasing dreams in line for bread,
Did I forget to wake up dead?

Socks don't match, my shirt's a mess,
I wonder if I'm cursed or blessed.
But here I am, with laughter's call,
Is there a point? I just can't stall.

Traffic jams and mundane chats,
Life's a circus filled with cats.
Juggling tasks, I trip and fall,
Yet somehow, I'm still having a ball.

So raise a glass to the routine,
To the absurd and all the unseen.
In this chaos, joy will grow,
Perhaps that's the point we know.

The Mirrors of Our Making

Mirrors reflect a quirky bunch,
Who's that smiling? Did you munch?
Finding flaws in every gaze,
Life's just an untold maze.

Pondering over lunch and fries,
Why do humans wear disguise?
Dancing like nobody's there,
Yet slipping on a virtual chair.

We chase the dreams that make us bold,
Twisting tales that never get old.
Winks and nods, we play the part,
But where's the script? Let's start from heart.

So here's to us in mirrors bright,
Reflecting laughter in soft twilight.
Maybe each crack's a special brew,
A toast to the odd, the funny, the true.

Echoes in the Labyrinth

Wandering through this endless maze,
Where's the exit? Lost in a daze.
Every corner echoes with cheer,
Or is that just my advance in beer?

Chasing shadows, feeling spry,
Talking to walls, oh my, oh my!
Each riddle takes a quirky twist,
In this conundrum, we persist.

Laughing ghosts from yesteryear,
Raise a toast, let's share some beer.
Why do we fret in this wild dance?
Let's just enjoy our frolicking chance!

So let the echoes fill the air,
With laughter that's beyond compare.
In this labyrinth, we shall find,
That fun's the truth we leave behind.

Sifting Through Stardust

Under the stars with a puzzled face,
Sifting through dust, what a strange place!
Is there meaning? Perhaps a clue,
Or are we just a cosmic stew?

Count the wishes, open your eyes,
Floating hopes wrap like fireflies.
What's the score in this silly game?
Winning feels a bit too lame.

We plot and plan, then slip on a dream,
Chasing the shimmer of what might gleam.
Don't sweat the small stuff, just stay bright,
Stardust tickles, and we take flight!

So here's the secret to all we seek,
Laughing at nonsense, it's not so bleak.
In the grand scheme, the punchline's clear,
Perhaps the point is simply here.

Reflections on a Fleeting Journey

We're all stuck in a loop, like a song on repeat,
Chasing our tails, downing fast food for a treat.
Wanderlust in our hearts, but the couch calls us back,
Netflix and snacks, on adventure we lack.

Got dreams of a trip to a road not yet paved,
But grocery lists and laundry make us feel enslaved.
We count down the minutes, till Friday arrives,
Then binge-watch the series, so nobody survives.

With maps in the drawer, we plan our escape,
Yet end up lost... in the fridge, with some grape.
The great outdoors waits, though we're shouting in vain,
'Just one more episode,' we mumble again.

So here's to the dreamers, the couch-bound parades,
Planning grand journeys while living in shades.
At the end of our quest, in slippers we'll sit,
And laugh at the places we almost did hit.

Moments That Might Have Been

At dawn of the day, we don our pretzel hats,
With visions of grandeur, we channel our cats.
'Look at us go!' we bravely exclaim,
Then trip on a shoelace, oh what a shame!

So many adventures we wished we could've braved,
Yet coffee and crumbs mean we're comfy and saved.
The big world outside can be scary, it's true,
But hey, who needs skydiving when snacks will do?

Invitations for parties come sending a thrill,
But often we'd rather just chill for the chill.
Hilarious stories we tell with a giggle,
While stubbornly holding our wine glasses, wiggle.

As each moment whizzes, like cars in a race,
We laugh at the chaos, and smile at our space.
For what are these tales but laughter's sweet spin?
In the end, we just smile at moments unseen.

The Dance of Impermanence

We twirl through the days like leaves in the wind,
Often clutching our coffee, too anxious to grin.
Just when we get serious, life plays a prank,
A shoe flies by, while we're lost in the tank.

Plans made with gusto dissolve like a puff,
Each turn of the page shows this rhythm is tough.
We think we're so clever, we march with a plan,
Then trip on a banana peel, as if it's a scam.

Time's a mischievous trickster, so sly and so bold,
Flipping our watches to moments of old.
The clock strikes twelve, and the cheese turns to dust,
While we dance with the chaos, maintaining our trust.

Let's frolic like children, though adults we pretend,
For in all this confusion, we can still find a friend.
We'll laugh until twilight and chase away dread,
For the dance of this whimsy is better than bed.

Shadows in the Quiet

In the silence we ponder, those thoughts never cease,
As shadows do wiggle, seeking knowledge and peace.
We wander through moments that tick softly by,
With asides that we share, like sparks in the sky.

A room filled with echoes, where laughter once lived,
In corners of comfort, life gives what it gives.
We sip on our tea, while the cat takes a leap,
Whiskers twitching wildly, in dreams so deep.

We search for the meaning, though donuts could suffice,
As sugar coats wisdom, and laughter's our vice.
With whiskers and whispers, indulging our plight,
The shadows of quiet bring out our delight.

So if pondering's heavy and burdens seem tall,
Just grab a good cookie, and have a small ball.
For in quiet reflections, we're never alone,
And the laughter we share turns the shadows to stone.

The Intersection of Paths

Two roads crossed with a sigh,
One said 'Go', the other 'Why?'
A signpost bent, just like my plan,
I think I'll wait for a better span.

A squirrel laughed as he ran by,
With an acorn stash, he looked so spry.
While I'm here caught in my own head,
He's busy plotting his mushroom spread.

Lost in thought as I stand still,
He scurried back with another thrill.
Paths may twist and turn and fret,
But I'm still here, and he's not wet.

So here I ponder, no real hurry,
While nature's critters dance in flurry.
Perhaps I'll join, take off this frown,
After all, it's just a silly town.

Silence Between Heartbeats

In the pause where worries stall,
I try to make sense, but then I sprawl.
A tick-tock clock with no real rhyme,
Says life's a joke, just a bit out of time.

Between heartbeats there's a gentle laugh,
Like waiting for coffee, that perfect half.
Just when I think I've found the clue,
The cat sits down, declaring 'It's true!'

A thought delays like a turtle in race,
I chase it round the kitchen space.
Yet in that quiet, a truth takes hold,
Life's the punchline of stories told.

So here I sit, with a half-baked pie,
Wondering what happens when I comply.
Silence rings but I just might shout,
It's all a riddle, without a doubt!

Crumpled Maps of Ambition

I unfurl my dreams, all wrinkles and hair,
With smudged-up lines that lead nowhere.
X marks the spot, or does it tease?
Perhaps it's just marking birdwatching cheese.

With coffee stains on plans never made,
I seek the path but have to evade.
A compass spins, much like my head,
Unfairly lost, yet not misled.

Ambition's a funny little thing indeed,
Like planting a garden, but where's the seed?
As I dig through dreams, I pull up a weed,
But maybe it's time to change my breed.

So I doodle plans on napkins galore,
With wit and whimsy, not grief in store.
Crumpled maps in my pocket will do,
For the journey's the joke, and I'm the view!

The Allure of the Unseen

Behind the curtain, what do I find?
A mirror reflecting my worried mind.
The allure of shadows, so sleek and sly,
Whispers of mischief that flutter and fly.

I once chased a dream that danced out of view,
While it giggled at me, saying 'Boo-hoo!'
Each turn a riddle, every pause a jest,
The unseen's a party I never could guess.

With socks unmatched and a hat for flair,
I plot my course through unseen air.
It tickles the fancy to wander about,
With the unseen muse, I mix up the rout.

So let's toast to what can't be known,
In foggy corners, we've always grown.
The unseen allure can giggle and tease,
And in that laughter, my heart finds ease.

The Palette of Existence

We paint our days with colors bright,
Yet wonder if it's wrong or right.
A splash of blue, a dash of red,
Is this the life we really led?

We mix the hues, we blend and swirl,
In our own art, we twirl and twirl.
But in the end, when brushes down,
Is anyone wearing a clown's crown?

The canvas stretches wide and vast,
Moments painted, shadows cast.
With every stroke, we laugh and cry,
As we debate the reason why.

Yet here we stand, both bold and meek,
With every color, we try to peek.
In this gallery of sheer delight,
We chase the meaning, with all our might.

Silent Conversations with Eternity

I chatted with time, a clownish gnome,
Who offered me a cupcake dome.
With sprinkles of wisdom and frosting of fate,
We chuckled through hours, us two, a crate.

He said, "Why worry? Just eat this slice,
The secrets of ages come with a price.
You'll find the answers between the crumbs,
And when you're done, the next one comes!"

The clock ticked on, quite unfazed,
I sipped my tea, and dreamily gazed.
Eternity winked, what a jolly tease,
I guess it's just here to give us a breeze.

So talk to the silence, you'll sometimes glean,
The trick is to laugh, and never be mean.
For in those quiet laughs lies a spark,
Of wisdom buried in the dark.

A Riddle Wrapped in Time

What is a riddle? A twisty fun game,
With answers looming, always the same.
A why wrapped in when, it's hard to unwind,
So we dance in circles, way behind.

They say the answer is found in a smile,
But mine seems to vanish after a while.
I scratch my head, and ponder so tough,
Is this existence made simply of fluff?

The clock counts down like a jester's joke,
Each tick a chuckle, each tock a poke.
So let us revel in this tricky charade,
And wear our confusion like a grand parade.

And while we unravel the enigma revealed,
Let's toast to the laughter, our fate sealed.
For the best riddle of all is to find,
That joy's the punchline—how beautifully blind!

The Fabric of Our Days

We weave our moments with threads of cheer,
Stitching up laughter, tackling our fear.
A patchwork quilt, all misfits combined,
In this crazy fabric, what will we find?

With needle and thread, we join the odd bits,
Like mismatched socks, or squishy split sits.
We iron out wrinkles, and fear not the fray,
Forever sewing our silly ballet.

Oh, these tangled skeins can drive us to shout,
Yet each little knot holds mysteries about.
So let's dance through the seams in our colorful ways,
Creating the tapestry that is our days.

For when buttons pop and the stitches come loose,
We laugh at the chaos, we've got the right juice.
So let's keep on weaving, with giggles and play,
As we hold up the fabric of our bright display.

The Quest for Hidden Truths

In search of answers, I lost my socks,
The universe laughs, playing clever tricks.
I ask the stars, they wink and twirl,
As I trip on questions in this wobbly whirl.

A wise old owl joins my silly dash,
With every clue, he just wants to laugh.
He hoots of fortune, but all I hear,
Is the sound of my snack bag, oh dear!

My compass spins, in ways so absurd,
Guiding my heart but never my words.
The path is twisted, like a pretzel's twist,
Finding more humor in the things I missed.

Yet here I stand, with wisdom so grand,
Collecting oddments from this quirky land.
For in the chase, hilarity reigns,
Each silly stumble, I boldly maintain.

The Colors of an Unfamiliar Dawn

Awake with colors that dance and blend,
A rainbow laugh, where shadows wend.
I painted my toast with zest and zeal,
But all I got was a surreal meal.

The sun peeks out, a cheeky spark,
Chasing giants as we stroll through the park.
The world spins round, in a whimsical sway,
As time trips over, and giggles away.

A flock of birds in pajamas fly,
Singing sweet nonsense to the blushing sky.
I join the chorus, my voice in disguise,
Turning life's puzzles into silly pies.

So let's toast to dawns with laughter and cheer,
In every hue that sparkles near.
For in every moment, absurd or grand,
Exists a giggle in this colorful land.

Mirages of Tomorrow

Tomorrow's dreams are wiggly things,
Like gummy worms with imaginary wings.
I reach for gold in the sand and sway,
But it slips through fingers, oh what a play!

A crystal ball spins, with glittery glee,
Showing visions of cats serving tea.
I shrug and ponder, what's meant to be,
In a world where whimsy runs free.

Each mirage winks as I trip through space,
I chase after futures at a snail's pace.
Laughter erupts like a bubble parade,
While I'm stuck wondering how I got played.

But still I dance, with sprinkles and cheer,
Embracing the nonsense, each fleeting year.
For in this jig, I find clarity's song,
That sometimes it's okay to be silly and wrong.

The Dance of the Infinite

In a waltz with questions that spin like a top,
I twirl on the edges, then suddenly drop.
The floor is a canvas, with paint galore,
As I shuffle through thoughts, who could want more?

A serendipitous tune fills the air,
While I pirouette through my most funny despair.
The cosmos chuckles, "Isn't this grand?"
With mismatched shoes and a ice cream cone band.

Each step I take, a giggle's perfume,
As the universe grins, dispelling the gloom.
In the shuffle of stars, I occasionally trip,
But life's dance of chaos is a luscious quip.

So let's laugh together, in this infinite spree,
As we glide past the silly, just you and me.
For in every stumble and every miss,
We find joy in the chaos, and endless bliss.

The Path of Wanderers

We stroll on paths, both wide and thin,
Chasing shadows, wearing grins.
With maps all upside down, we roam,
Lost in thought, we're far from home.

Each step a dance, a silly feat,
Dodging puddles, oh, what a treat!
From left to right, we twirl and swirl,
Turning life's chaos into a whirl.

We ponder questions, big and small,
Like where is Jimmy? Who named the wall?
In a world that spins, we keep it bright,
With laughter loud, we take flight.

So here we wander, no end in sight,
With snack breaks planned, our hearts feel light.
A journey shared, with friends so dear,
Through twists and turns, we persevere.

Fragile Threads of Connection

We weave our bonds with threads so fine,
Stumbling often on shared punchlines.
Each giggle sparks a new design,
In this tapestry, oh so divine.

With coffee spills and memes galore,
We find our joy in the craziest lore.
Like socks that disappear in the wash,
Our connections thrive, even when posh.

We feel the tug of friendship's art,
A funny story that warms the heart.
Through tangled jokes, we find our way,
As fragile threads keep worries at bay.

So here's to moments all woven tight,
In chaos and laughter, we find our light.
Beneath the mess, love leaves a trace,
In threads of connection, we find our place.

Beneath the Laughter

Behind the chuckles, there's truth to seek,
A quirky angle in every peak.
With every LOL and rolling eye,
We search for meaning while we fly high.

We tickle thoughts that dance away,
As we ponder why we're here each day.
With silly hats and goofy stunts,
We chase the why, and laugh in fronts.

Through jest and jive, we try to cope,
With jokes about cake and tiny hope.
Each snicker hides a nugget wise,
In laughter's balm, our spirit flies.

So under laughter's wondrous sway,
We stumble forward, come what may.
Embrace the fun, and let it flow,
For in the giggles, deeper truths grow.

A Tear

A single tear, or maybe two,
Slips down with laughter, who even knew?
It rolls like a marble, round and bold,
Among the giggles, stories unfold.

In moments grand, it turns to jest,
A slip on the floor, we're all quite blessed.
So here's to tears, let's have some more,
For every fumble opens a door.

We laugh at woes that seem so dire,
With silly hats, we'll never tire.
In every drop, a lesson clear,
To hold each moment, laugh through the tears.

So let them flow, those sparkling falls,
We'll gather them up in laughter's halls.
For in this dance of joy and fright,
We find our way to love and light.

Embracing the Unfathomable

In the vast unknown, we touch the sky,
With questions that make a wise man sigh.
We spin in circles, chasing our tails,
Unraveling puzzles with crazy gales.

So wear your frown like a shiny crown,
Embrace the wild, and turn it around.
With puzzled looks and coffee in hand,
We're all just trying to understand.

Through cosmic giggles and silly plots,
We juggle dreams like steaming pots.
So what's the meaning? It's hard to tell,
But let's enjoy this joker's spell!

For in the midst of all the strife,
We peek and poke at this wobbly life.
With laughter loud, we join the dance,
Embrace the ride, and take a chance.

Beneath the Surface of Time

Tick-tock goes the clock, what a race,
Chasing our tails in a frantic pace.
We juggle our tasks, in a whimsical show,
Yet can't find the time for a leisurely glow.

The fish in the sea wear watches on fins,
Calculating slowly while counting their sins.
They laugh at our rush, swimming 'round like a breeze,
While we're stuck on land, caught up in disease.

So look at the tides, how they ebb and they flow,
Try moving your feet in the sand's sweet tableau.
A wink from the sky, a nudge from the ground,
Embrace the absurdity, humor astound.

In this circus of time, what do we defend?
A laugh with your lunch, a hug from a friend.
The seconds we fret, the minutes that fly,
It's often the giggles that help us get by.

The Riddles of Being

Why do we wake, and why do we sleep?
Questions like these could make a cat weep.
Do socks go to heaven, or just disappear?
Like tidbits of wisdom that vanish from here.

We ponder our snacks, both salty and sweet,
As life offers puzzles for us to defeat.
Yet all of this thought takes a terrible toll,
When the cheese on your nachos is burnt on a roll.

Do trees have their secrets? They stand bold and tall.
What do they whisper when leaves start to fall?
Perhaps it's a riddle, they groove with the breeze,
To teach us the point, despite feeling unease.

So laugh at the quirks, take each riddle with cheer,
For the answers you seek might just not be here.
Embrace the unknown, and dance in the rain,
In the end, it's the giggles that keep us sane.

Dance of the Ephemeral

The butterflies flit, with grace in their flight,
While we trip on our shoelaces, what a sight!
They hum a soft tune, as if in the know,
While we struggle for purpose in life's dizzy show.

With bubbles in hand, we dream and we spin,
About fancy careers or the chaos within.
Yet what if the joy rests in giggles and glee,
In toasting the winds with a nice cup of tea?

So on each wobbly step, let's twirl with delight,
And laugh at our faints in the flickering light.
For the dance of today could vanish like mist,
And leave us with giggles in sweet, silly bliss.

The colors of moments, a vibrant parade,
With each twist and turn, it's the laughter we've made.
So join in the waltz, hold your partner so tight,
In this dance of the fleeting, let's laugh through the night.

Shadows of a Distant Dream

In shadows we linger, draped like a cape,
Sipping on dreams, making escapes.
What if tomorrow is just silly play?
With clowns and confetti to brighten the gray?

Our worries like fog on a windy old street,
Always getting tangled in nonsensical heat.
Yet look at the sky, such splendid delight,
Even clouds have their punchlines; just take a bite!

So here's to the jesters, the fools in the fold,
They gather our laughter; it's magic, not mold.
Take heed of the glimmers, the beams that ignite,
For the shadows just twinkle when dressed in moonlight.

So dance in your dreams, let your worries unwind,
Find laughter and joy in the silly and blind.
For in this grand circus, we're all juggling balls,
And sometimes the punchline is the best of them all.

Through the Lens of Curiosity

Why do ducks wear yellow shoes?
They waddle like they own the street.
We ponder hard on cosmic blues,
While munching snacks and counting sheep.

Thoughts bounce around like ping-pong balls,
We ask, but answers seem to flee.
In life's circus, a jester calls,
With pies and laughter, set us free.

The fridge hums a curious tune,
While socks mysteriously disappear.
We chase shadows by the light of the moon,
And giggle at what we hold dear.

So grab a drink and toast to jest,
For all our questions, just a game.
The search for meaning isn't a test,
It's more like a riddle: who's to blame?

Navigating the Sea of Questions

Why do fish seem to swim in schools?
Do they have secret learning plans?
A dolphin winks, while swimming fools,
Texting seagulls, making new fans.

What's deeper, the ocean or our thoughts?
Do lobsters dream of spicy fries?
Diving into ideas like untapped pots,
With shrimp as guides, we reach for the skies.

The tide pulls back, our doubts arise,
Yet crabs provide their own wisdom.
In shells they hide, without goodbyes,
We chuckle at their wonky kingdom.

Sailing on the waves of silly grips,
We find the humor in our plight.
With seaweed laughs and salty quips,
Our journey's brightened by delight.

The Conundrum of Being

Why do we trip over air we swear?
Maybe gravity's just messing with us.
A butterfly flits with utmost flair,
While we're busy finding our own bus.

Existence feels like a game of charades,
Where the prize is a slice of pie.
We juggle thoughts like circus parades,
And giggle as the clowns pass by.

Do ants discuss their work-life stress?
Or is it just us, always in a rush?
We ponder hard, then feel the mess,
And laugh at all our silly hush-hush.

So dance with questions, let them sway,
In the rhythm of absurd delight.
Who needs answers? Just join the play,
Finding joy in the strange insight.

Beyond the Horizon of Expectation

Why do we think we're here to plan?
The cat seems to know what's the deal.
As we mix our drinks and make a stand,
Felines lounge while we spin the wheel.

Expectations float like balloons in flight,
Some pop, others drift out to sea.
We giggle at dreams that take a bite,
As we munch on popcorn, carefree.

Chasing ambitions like they're grand meals,
Naming dishes we'll never make.
With sauce and puns, the humor reveals,
Oh, what a silly, delightful mistake!

So raise a glass to the unknown ground,
To futures bright and futures strange.
For in the twists of fun, we're bound,
To laugh at how quickly thoughts can change.

Chasing the Flicker of Meaning

In a world where socks do hide,
We search for purpose, though we bide.
With cereal mixed for breakfast treats,
We ponder why we're on these streets.

The cat gives wisdom, napping tight,
While outside, birds sing with delight.
We chase the flicker, lose the flame,
As life's wild ride just plays its game.

A rubber duck floats by our side,
In the deep pool of thoughts we glide.
We trip on dreams, but laugh it off,
And dance with joy rather than scoff.

So raise a glass to all our fears,
For meaning's hid in laughter, cheers!
A silly joke, or smile, or glance,
In the absurd, let's swirl and dance.

The Illusion of Certainty

A plan is set, or so we think,
But coffee spills, and pens do clink.
We lay our tracks, but trains go rogue,
The map's a joke, just like our vogue.

In meetings dull, we chase the facts,
While daydreams soar on comfy backs.
What's solid ground? A sneaky jest,
With all our quirks, we feel quite blessed.

We argue points, so proud, so bright,
Then trip on air—a silly sight.
The grand designs, we try to cast,
Just jokes we tell, as moments pass.

So here's to chaos in the line,
The twists and turns we dare define.
With laughter loud, we ditch the fright,
In absurdity, we find our light.

Hues of an Unwritten Journey

An unwritten tale we try to spin,
With crayons bright and goofy grins.
The road ahead, a prism wide,
Where every turn's a bumpy ride.

We dream in shades of rogue delight,
With pumpkins misplaced in the moonlight.
Each step is drawn in vivid hue,
In this wild play, we sketch what's true.

A twist of fate, a wobbly jump,
In life's own circus, we join the frump.
With colors smeared upon the page,
We laugh at fate—what a lovely stage!

So paint your thoughts with daring flair,
In the mess of art, find joy to share.
With every hue, embrace the strange,
In the chaos, let your story change.

The Lament of the Lost Poets

Oh, gather 'round, dear lost brigade,
As we lament this strange charade.
The verses run like socks in wash,
With meaning blurred, we empathize with the posh.

In hopes of prose, we stumble neat,
With rhymes that chaotically defeat.
Yet in the fray of every line,
We find some fun, and it's just divine.

With quirky tales and joyful glee,
We wonder what our words might free.
The poets lost, in fits and starts,
Write riddles rich with quirky parts.

So let us cheer for scattered pens,
For witty lines and jolly friends.
In every failure, fun reveals,
A truth that's crafted in our feels.

The Symphony of Being

With every tick, the clock goes boom,
We dance around, avoiding gloom.
We trip on fate, we trip on toes,
Yet somehow still, the laughter grows.

A sandwich here, a sock misplaced,
Life's little quirks, a funny taste.
We chase our dreams in silly hats,
While plotting schemes with dogs and cats.

A dance of chaos, a whirl of cheer,
We rustle through the yesteryear.
Through tangled hair and silly jokes,
We may just be the universe's folks.

In this big show, we play our part,
A funny dance, a quirky art.
So raise a glass, let's toast it right,
For all the wrongs, we'll make it bright.

In Search of the Elusive Why

Why wear shoes with holes and stains?
Why sing to the moon in silly refrains?
We ponder deep while munching fries,
   The answer hides behind the pies.

We chase our tails, we ask the cat,
In hopes of finding where we're at.
With each new question, coffee spills,
   Oh, the lost hours, oh, the thrills!

So here we stand, on wobbly ground,
Like sentient plants that dance around.
Through trails of laughter, we may find,
   The meaning's just to be unlined.

Perhaps it's not a grand big score,
But giggles shared, and so much more!
Let's skip along this puzzling road,
   And celebrate our silly code!

The Echo of Existence

In halls of Echo, we cry and jest,
"What's the point?" We jest with zest.
Mirror, mirror, on the wall,
Who's the silliest of them all?

With rubber chickens and foam pie fights,
We wander through the fun-filled nights.
We scribble woes on napkin scrolls,
And dance with socks—yes, that's our goals!

The echoes bounce, they skip, they sway,
Like wildflowers on a sunny day.
In every blunder and goof we make,
A bit of joy's the prize we take.

So join the beat, let laughter ring,
In this nutty world, we are the king!
With silly love, we paint it bright,
The echoes of us, a pure delight.

The Quest for Meaning

With capes made of towels and plastic swords,
We embark on journeys, cross all boards.
We question all the quirks we meet,
While dancing barefoot in the street.

Climbing trees, we search for signs,
Cardboard crowns and makeshift shrines.
Through windy paths and ice cream cones,
We giggle and laugh, and we make the phones!

The treasure chest filled with silly dreams,
Golden giggles and bubbling streams.
In pudding cups, we carve our truth,
With sprinkles bright, to proclaim our youth.

So grab a friend, let's chase the chase,
In this wild game, there's much to embrace.
For meaning lies in all we share,
In every glimmer of quirky flair.

Threads of Uncertainty

With socks that rarely match, we roam,
In closets full of chaos, our happy home.
The laundry spins like dreams untold,
A fashion statement in bright and bold.

We ponder life's great complex maze,
Where ramen noodles win the culinary praise.
Between lost keys and wayward shoes,
We dance through awkward, blissful blues.

With coffee spilled and pizza crust,
In laughter and mishaps, we find trust.
As dawn breaks with its golden hue,
We shrug and smile, what else to do?

So let us twirl in this grand ballet,
Where humor and madness come out to play.
In threads of uncertainty, we weave and dance,
Embracing the silly, we take our chance.

The Pursuit of the Enigmatic

Why do we chase those fleeting dreams?
Like cats in shadows, or fish in streams.
With questions marked in ponderous ink,
We consume our thoughts, we barely think.

To seek the truth, we'll run and race,
Yet trip on banana peels, a common face.
Curiosity, our hovercraft,
In a world where answers prompt a gaffe.

The clock ticks loudly, drives us mad,
And searching for meaning can feel quite bad.
But with a wink and a crooked grin,
We giggle at chaos, where joy begins.

What if the secret's a simple trick?
A dash of humor, a clever flick.
In this pursuit, we play the jest,
Life's riddle might just be a quirky quest.

Fleeting Moments

In moments fast like ice cream drips,
We chase the giggles, the funny quips.
A sneeze at dinner, a slip on ice,
These fleeting gems are oh so nice.

With every laugh, a tickled soul,
In stumbles and snorts, we find our role.
We dance with time as it whirls away,
Embracing absurdity without dismay.

Chocolate crumbs on our hopeful face,
We lose the race but win the chase.
With each odd moment that catches breath,
We laugh at the thrill and tease out death.

So gather the moments, let laughter reign,
For in silly mischief, there's joy to gain.
These fleeting flashes make life a blast,
A whirlwind of smiles, forever to last.

Endless Questions

Is the toaster a time machine, I wonder?
Will socks ever find their way back from plunder?
In a world where logic takes a nap,
We flip through life in a comical flap.

Do fish ever get thirsty, humor me,
Or is it just us, chained to the sea?
The meerkat dances, the parrot squawks,
We ponder the mysteries as the clock ticks o'clock.

Why can't we pet the internet cat?
And what's the deal with a pumpkin hat?
In endless questions, we find our zest,
As giggles emerge from this timeless quest.

So here's to the puzzles, both silly and grand,
In the chaos of questions, together we stand.
For life, it seems, is a jolly jest,
An endless riddle in a whimsical quest.

Reflections in a Broken Mirror

Each crack in glass tells tales untamed,
Of glamorous mornings, or nights unnamed.
With a wink to my reflection, I laugh and grin,
At the funny faces shaped from within.

A crooked nose, a wild hairdo,
Who knew a remnant could seem so new?
In shards of stories, we find our glow,
Through laughter and flaws, we learn to grow.

So let's toast to chaos, the ups and downs,
To lost keys, wild dreams, and laughter crowns.
In broken mirrors, we find our art,
The beauty of madness, a world apart.

So break the glass, and take a chance,
In reflections of life, we dare to dance.
For in every crack, there's joy and fun,
Together we'll laugh, until we're done.

In the Heart of the Unknown

In shadows deep, we frolic and play,
As questions swirl like leaves in the fray.
Why are we here? A cosmic joke?
Maybe we're just a glitch in folk's smoke.

We chase our tails like dogs in a race,
Hoping to find a more sensible place.
Is it all just a game, a merry charade?
With laughter and whimsy, let's not be dismayed!

In search of the light, we stumble around,
Falling like clowns without making a sound.
The truth lies hidden, behind all the laughs,
And perhaps we're just comic book drafts!

So let us toast to this curious ride,
With quirks and quirks as our trusted guide.
The unknown's our friend, let's embrace the fun,
In this grand circus, we're all number one!

The Puzzles We Call Home

With jigsaw pieces all scattered about,
We search for the edge, but there's plenty of doubt.
Missing corners and shapes that don't fit,
A puzzle of chaos, yet we laugh and we sit.

We trade our socks for a slice of the pie,
Wondering why it's so hard just to fly.
Life's like a Rubik's, turning round and round,
But who needs answers when laughter's profound?

Is it the pizza or what's on the side?
Perhaps it's the toppings we can't seem to decide.
We mix up our plans like salad in a bowl,
Creating a mess—oh, what a grand goal!

Yet despite all the puzzles, both large and small,
Each chuckle can lead us past any wall.
So here's to the journey, the quirky, the wild,
In this pitiful chaos, we remain just a child!

In Search of the Unseen

With binoculars pointed at stars up above,
We scan for the answers, searching for love.
What's hiding behind that insipid façade?
Could it be cake? Oh, let's give a nod!

We scour the corners of whimsy and fun,
Hoping to find that elusive 'someone.'
In shadows we peek, wearing hats that are tall,
What's more crucial—who cares, after all?

As we dance through the fog and wander the street,
Perhaps what we seek is a warm cup of tea.
With laughter our compass, we'll navigate through,
The unseen's just silly, with giggles in view!

So grab your magnifying glass, here we go!
Onward to giggles, not a dull show!
For in seeking the unseen, we will just sigh,
And toast to the moments that make our hearts fly!

The Untold Stories of Us

In a realm of whispers, we keep it all tight,
With stories that twinkle like stars in the night.
Who's got the gossip? The tales that we spin?
Like cats telling secrets in the depths of our sin.

We gather in circles, with snacks piled high,
Sharing our fables, giving truth the sly eye.
Each tale more absurd than the last one we told,
Stretched like taffy, but warmth can't be sold!

Our sitcoms unfold beneath moonlit skies,
With mishaps and giggles, and the occasional sighs.
So here's to our stories, both wild and a bit,
In the book of our lives, we all play a skit!

With laughter as glue, we'll bind them with zest,
Our tales may be crazy, but they're simply the best.
In the untold chapters, the funny, the crude,
We find all the treasures that keep our hearts glued!

www.ingramcontent.com/pod-product-compliance
Lightning Source LLC
Chambersburg PA
CBHW072148200426
43209CB00051B/860